David and Goliath

First box set edition, 2015

Sky Pony Press books may be purchased in bulk at special discounts for sales promotion, corporate gifts, fund-raising, or educational purposes. Special editions can also be created to specifications. For details, contact the Special Sales Department, Sky Pony Press, 307 West 36th Street, 11th Floor, New York, NY 10018 or info@skyhorsepublishing.com.

Sky Pony® is a registered trademark of Skyhorse Publishing, Inc.®, a Delaware corporation.

Visit our website at www.skyponypress.com.

10 9 8 7 6 5 4 3 2 1

Manufactured in China, May 2015
This product conforms to CPSIA 2008

Library of Congress has cataloged the hardcover trade edition as follows:

Smith, Brendan Powell.
David and Goliath : the brick Bible for kids / Brendan Powell Smith.
pages cm
ISBN 978-1-62087-982-5 (hardcover : alk. paper) 1. David, King of Israel--Juvenile literature. 2. Goliath (Biblical giant)--Juvenile literature. 3. LEGO toys--Juvenile literature. I. Title.
BS580.D3S49 2013
222'.4309505--dc23
2013012071

Cover design by Brian Peterson
Cover photo credit Brendan Powell Smith

Slipcase ISBN: 978-1-63450-208-5
Ebook ISBN: 978-1-62873-352-5

Editor: Julie Matysik
Designer: Brian Peterson
Production Manager: Abigail Gehring

David and Goliath

THE BRICK BIBLE for Kids

Brendan Powell Smith

Sky Pony Press
New York

God's people, the Israelites, were at war with the Philistines.

The army of each nation stood facing each other, ready for battle.

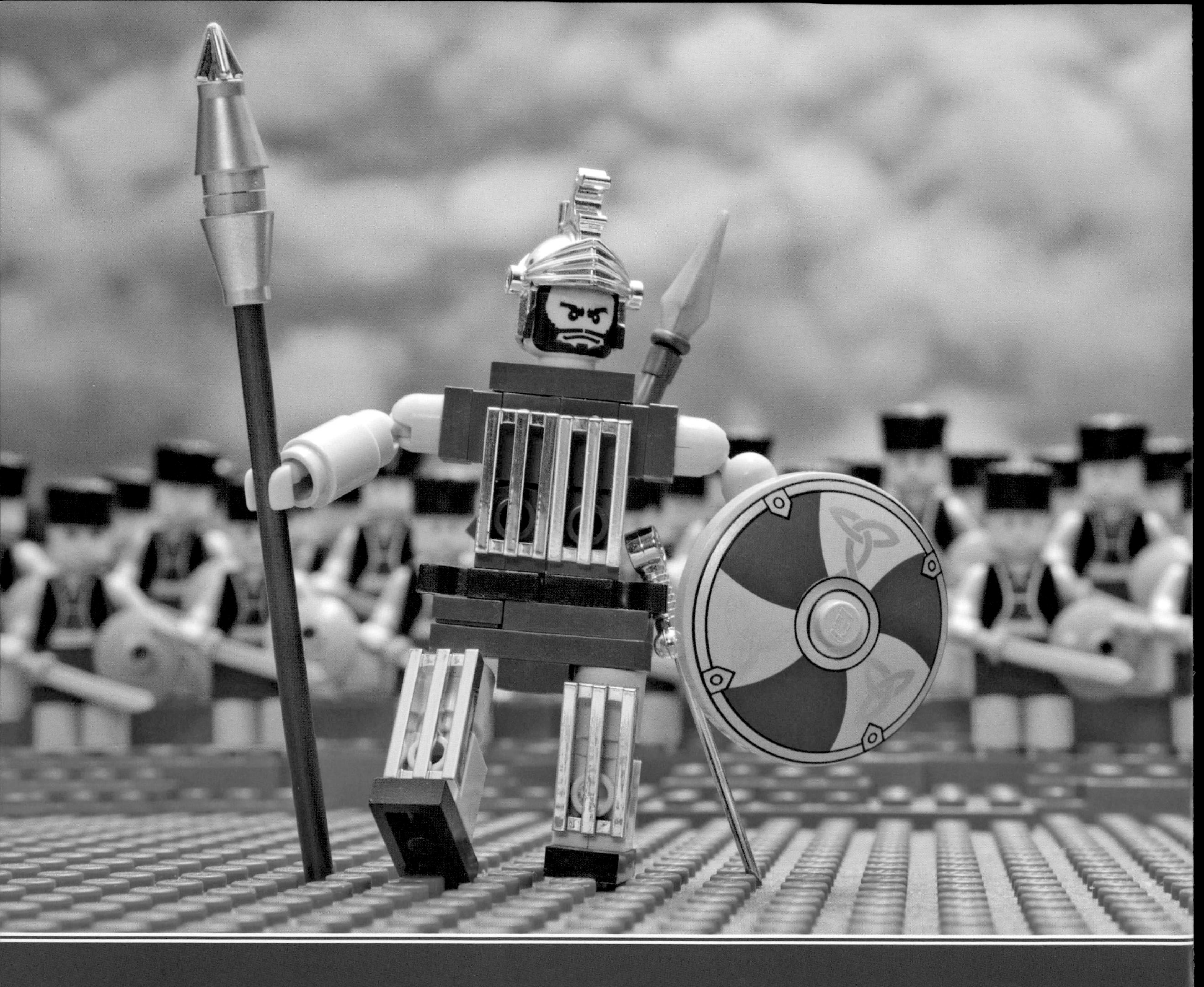

Among the Philistines was a giant named Goliath.
He carried a huge spear and shield
and wore a bronze helmet and armor.

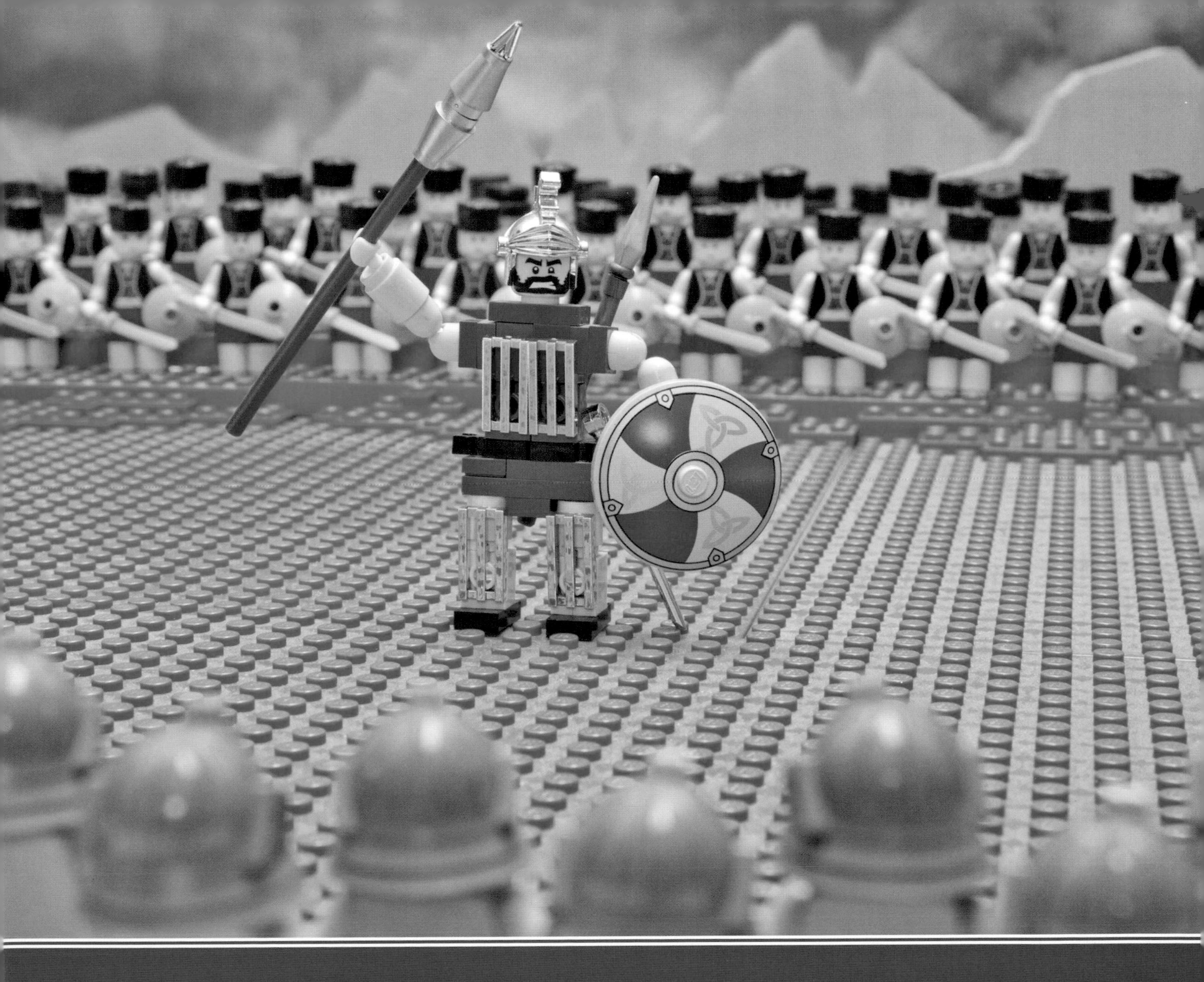

Goliath made a challenge to the Israelites, saying, “Send one of your men out to fight me. If he defeats me, we will be become your slaves. If I defeat him, you will become our slaves.”

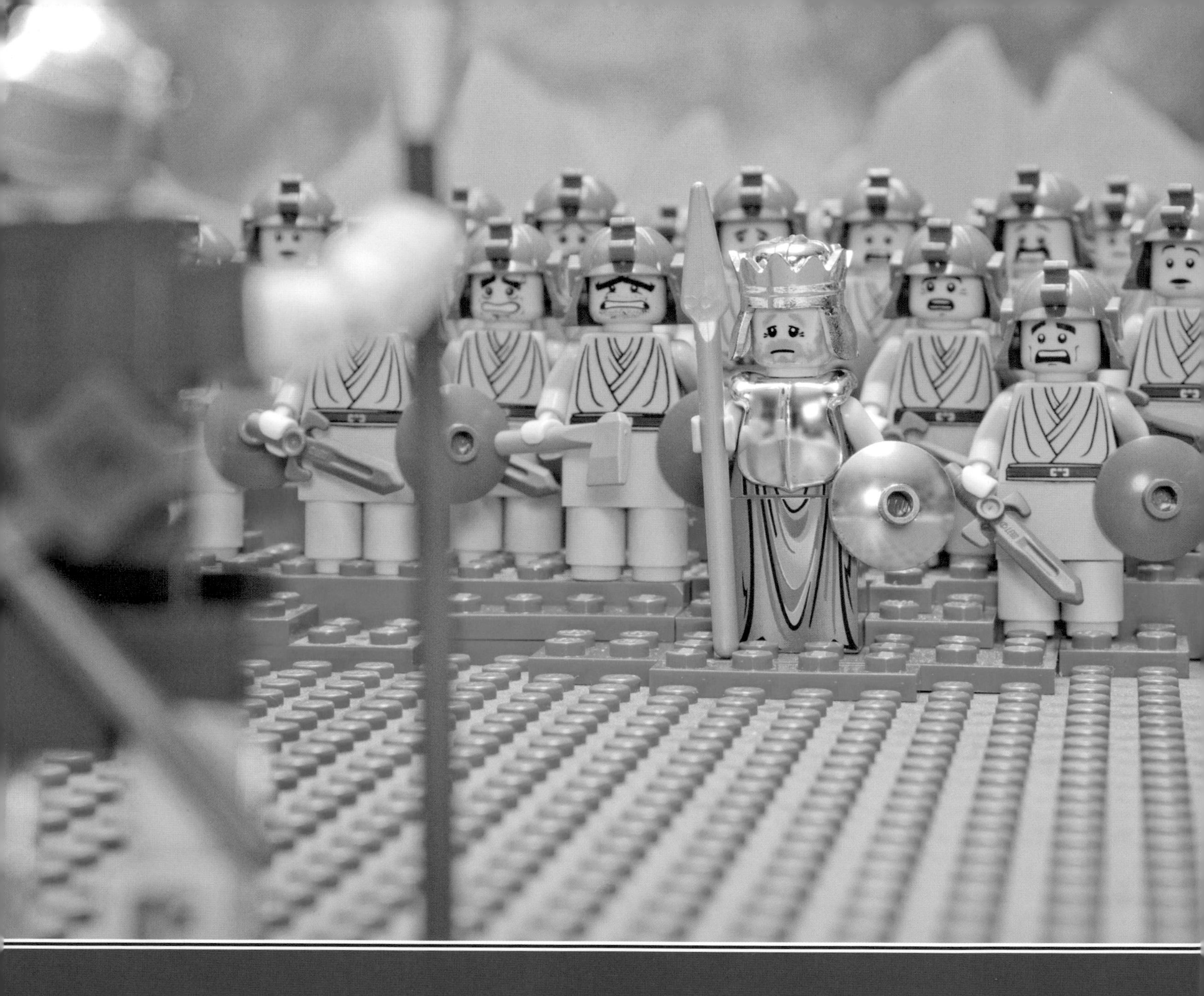

When they heard this, King Saul and the Israelites were terrified!

Miles away, in the town of Bethlehem, an Israelite boy named David was busy watching over his father's sheep, keeping them safe.

If a lion or a bear tried to eat one of the sheep,
David would chase after it.

He would grab it by the neck and strike it dead.

That day, however, David's father said to him, "Take this bread and this cheese to your older brothers in the army. See how they are doing and return to me with news."

So David traveled to where the army was preparing for battle. He left the bread and cheese with the supply keeper and ran to the front lines to find his brothers.

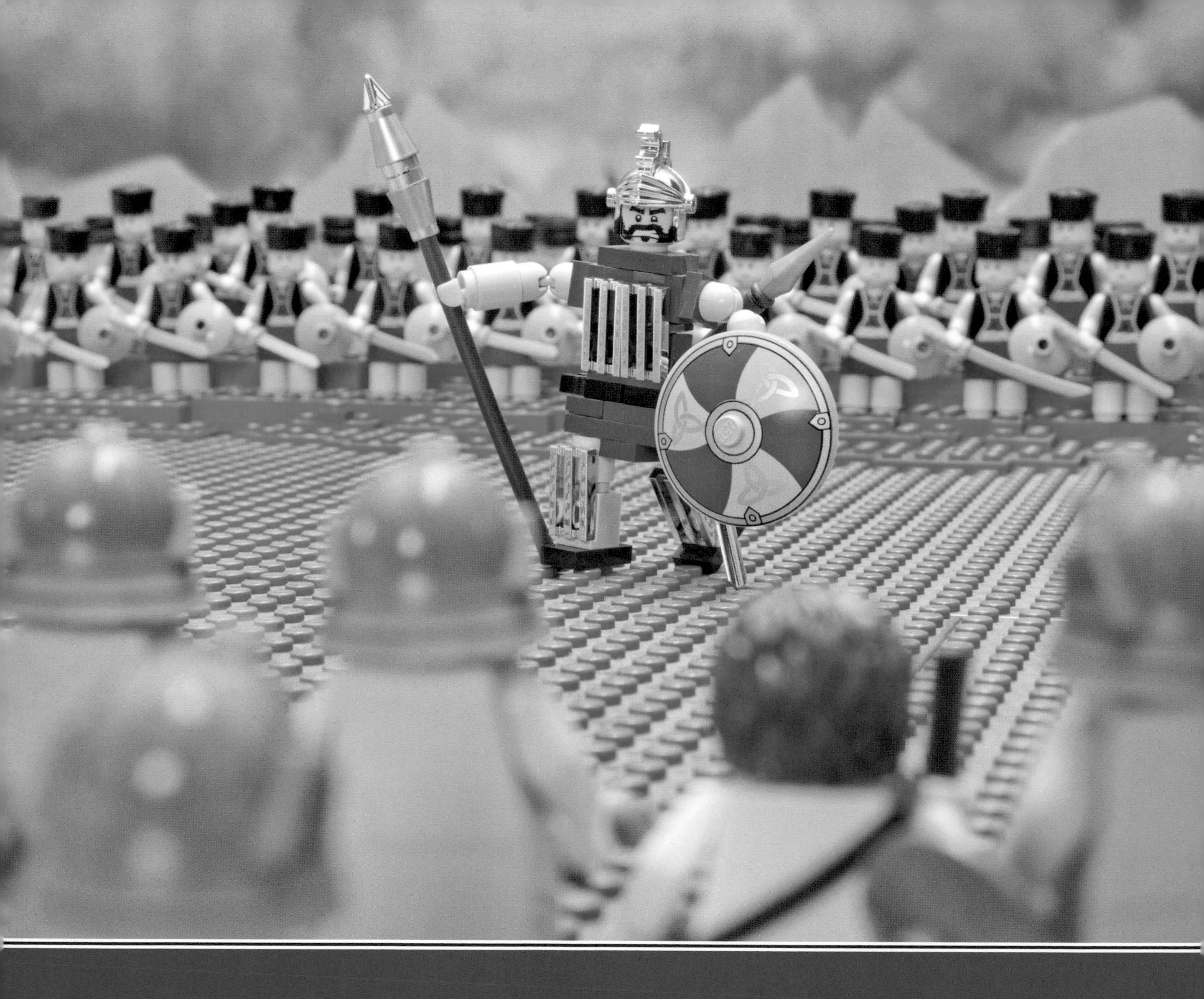

Just then, Goliath again stepped forward to challenge the Israelites, saying, “Send one of your men out to fight me.” And David heard this.

David asked the men standing near him, "What reward will be given to the man who kills this Philistine?" And they told him, "The King will give him great riches, and he will get to marry the princess."

David went to King Saul and said, “I will go out and fight this Philistine.” But King Saul told him, “You are just a boy, and the giant has been a warrior all his life! You can’t fight him!”

David told King Saul, “God protected me when I killed lions and bears, and God will protect me when I kill this giant who has challenged God’s army.”

King Saul said to David, "Go then, and may God be with you!" He gave David his royal armor and his sword and shield. But David said, "I can't walk like this! I'm not used to these things."

David took off all the armor and went to a stream to gather some smooth stones. He put them in his pockets.

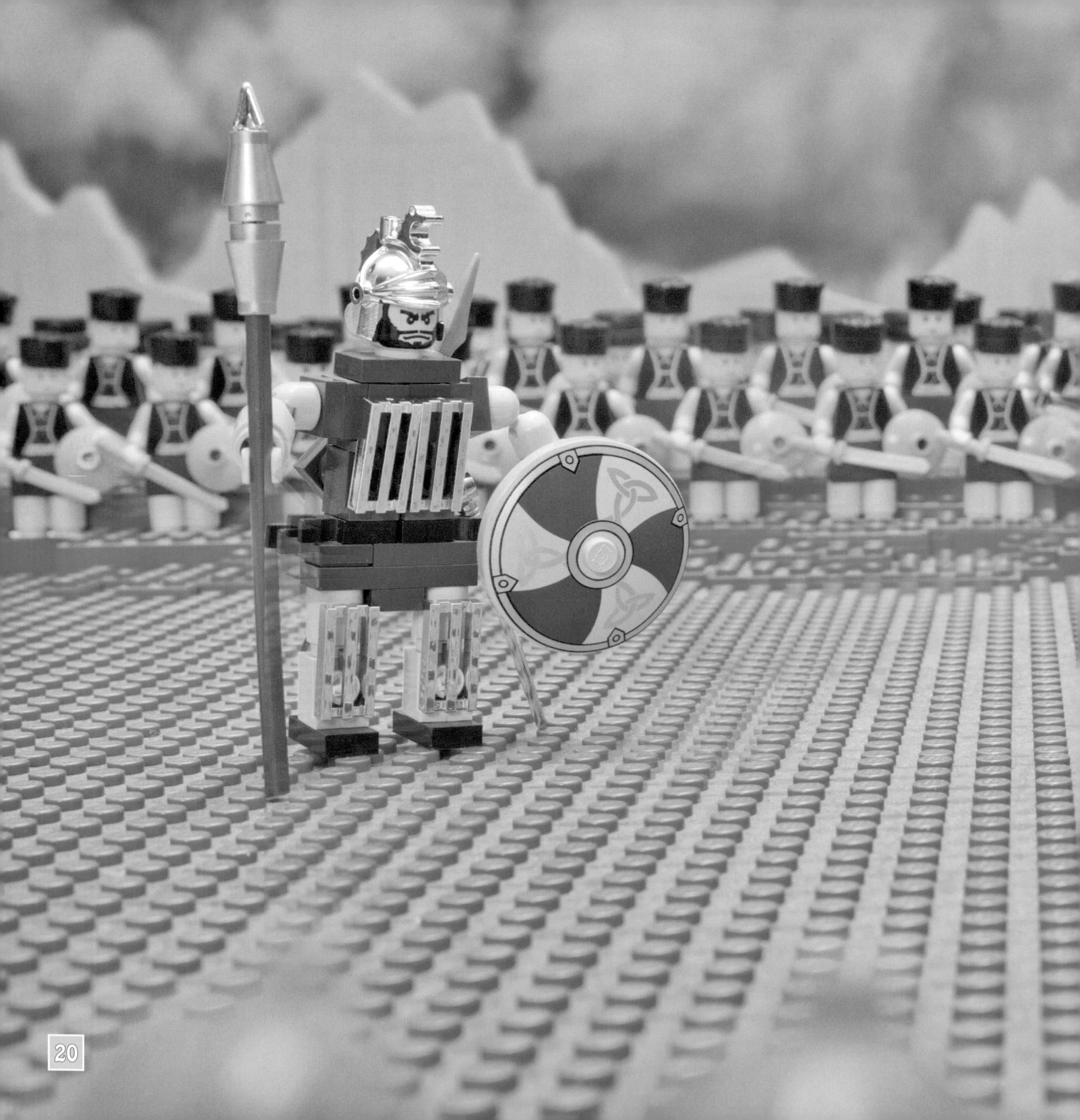

Carrying only his walking stick and a sling,
David went out to face Goliath the giant.

Goliath was insulted to see that such a small boy had come out to fight him. He said to David, “Do you think I am merely a dog? Is this why you come at me with a stick?”

But David said to him, “I have God on my side, and you have chosen to fight God’s army. Today I will kill you and cut off your head.”

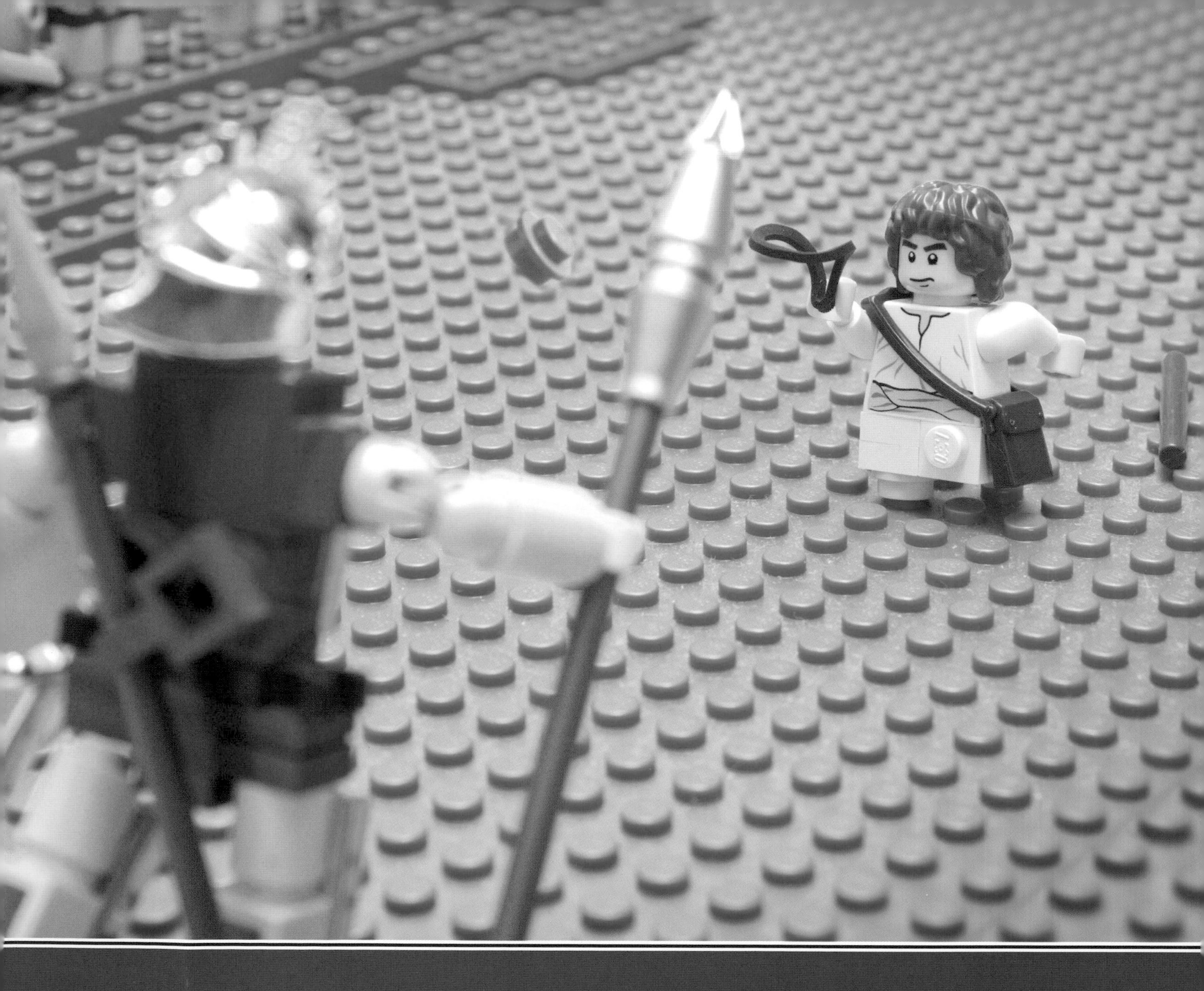

Goliath got angry and moved closer to attack. David took a stone from his pocket and used his sling to launch it at the giant.

The stone hit Goliath in the forehead.

Goliath fell down dead. David took the giant's sword and cut off his head.

When the Philistines saw that their champion was dead, they ran away in fear.

The Israelites chased after them and killed many of the Philistines that day.
Then the Israelites collected the food and the weapons left behind by the Philistines.

David took the head of Goliath to Jerusalem.
The people of Israel treated him as a hero and
sang songs to praise him.

When David grew up, he married King Saul's daughter, the princess Michal.

And God chose David to be the next King of Israel.

Activity!

Can you find these ten brick pieces in the book?
On which page does each appear?
The answers are below.

Answer key:

A: p.8, B: p.29, C: p.13, D: p.30, E: pp.28 and 30, F: p.16, G: p.19, H: p.12, I: p.17, J: p.12